Thirty Souls

by MCP North, Class of 2026

☀Rebirth Ink
Consulting & Publishing
Milwaukee, WI

Dedication

We would like to dedicate these poems to all of our mothers. We are dedicating this to them because without them, we would not be on earth. We would also like to dedicate our poems to them because without their inspiration we would not be so bright. Moms, thank you for blessing us!

The Authors:

Zaria Harris
Xavier Anderson
Drenyah Gentry
Lynnisha Carson
Angus Poston
Landon Lazenby
Zai'Quon Green
Mark Chambers
A'Drion Weston
Markayla Qualls
Josiah Payne
Keiora Sanders
Zakiya Tucker
Ty'Marius Jackson
Ja'Zayel Abboud
Natalie Taylor
Nyrice Barren
Jamela Brown-Davidson
Tony Racanelli
Domonic Allen
Jaiden Beason
Tha'Resa Alexander
Jodee Johnson
Kimani Nash
Andrell Kelley
Lashaya Tatum-Miller
Sydney Purifoy-Mahone
Kiyla Vasquez
Kailyn Britton-Henning

Introduction
By: Angus and Natalie

In the beginning of 2017, our class was was behaving like bunch of beef-brains. During the year, we showed a lot of growth, though. We have grown very mature throughout the fourth-grade. Even though we have grown a lot, we still have a long way to go.

In some ways we have grown a lot. We have improved on our writing, division, and reading fluency. We still need to improve on our behavior, but we are getting our act together (or at least trying to).

Our teachers are helping us make these improvements. One of them is Mrs. Forte. She tells the truth so much, it sounds like she is preaching. Ms. Sutherland, on the other hand, is very (very) strict. Then, on other days, we make her so happy, she is just.... well..... NICE (and not strict).

This is a collection of ORIGINAL poetry from both of our fourth grade classes. We have been inspired by listening to Popcorn, and other spoken word artists we heard in our ELA class. Some of us wrote about our lives and personal experiences, while others of us wrote about other people or situations we've seen in the world.

Our class has grown so much since 2017. It is a new time, and a new time means a new US. We *ARE* the fifth grade class now (well, almost!).

FROM THE WAKANDA CLASS of 2026

Fisk University BULLDOGS
&
University of Wisconsin-Oshkosh TITANS

I AM

By: Zaria Betty-Jean Harris

You say I am ugly

I say I am beautiful

You say I am dumb

I say I am smart

You say I am nothing

I say I am something

You say I am useless

I say I am useful

You say I am not

I say I am

So you are wrong I am something

So I can be anything if I put my mind to it

Help

By: Xavier Anderson

Deep down inside

No one can hear me

I am not seen

I am not heard

Still

I will rise to the top

Once I am seen

I will be happy

And things that you do

Should come from the heart

So that is where I will start

With the heart

I can be whoever I choose

My own rules

Even when I am upset

I do my best

Don't Judge A Book By Its Cover

By: Drenyah Marie Gentry

My teachers are really close friends

one is white and one is black.

If one says no they both say no.

You should never judge a person by their color.

Cause karma is a fool.

She will kill you and you won't even know it.

You don't know what that person is going through

cause when you get older

you gon be scrubbing their floors.

Me and my Dad

By: Lynnisha Lafay Carson

Me and my dad eat

Me and my dad play

Me and my dad tell jokes

Me and my dad laugh

Me and my dad play

I love my Dad

Night Light

By: Angus Poston

When the sun goes down
The night is still very bright
For the moon is my night light.

When the sun goes down
The stars come up
The sun is bright, too,
But not bright enough...

When the sun goes down
I leave off the light
Because the moon is just
too bright.

**NOW THAT IS ONE
AMAZING NIGHT
LIGHT!**

Bullying

By: Landon Lazenby and Zai'Quon Green

BULLYING is not funny or fun

people that BULLY think it is,

But it's not

Make sure you don't be a BULLY

If you see someone getting BULLIED

Don't watch

Speak up and help them

Friends

By: Mark Chambers

Friends are the glue that hold your darkness and light together

sometimes they make you do something stupid

and sometimes they stop you

sometimes they play with you

sometimes they don't

but even if they don't, they're still your friends

sometimes friendships can fall

sometimes they can build

but when you're friends with someone

you treat them right

and if you don't your friendship will fall

this is my experience with friends

it may not happen to you

but just in case, treat your friends right.

Anger

By: A'Drion Weston

I feel mad

And

When I get mad

I ball up my fist

Sometimes my friends make me mad

And

When I need to calm down

I have my two wonderful teachers here to help

And

I have my office mom

To help me calm down too

And

Sometimes I communicate

But

I will work on that

And

I will try to keep my emotions in control

And

I will keep working hard.

Sadness

By: Markayla Qualls

I feel sadness

When I am alone

I feel sadness

When nobody loves me

I feel sadness

When nobody cares about me

Now you know how I feel

Joy

By: Josiah Payne

I feel happy
I feel sad
People make me happy
People make me sad

I make myself happy
I make myself joyful
I don't think about the people
That make me sad

I don't worry about them
I just put joy in them
I am nice
Not mean

So I can make my own dreams
I can do many things
So I can be a star
And go very far

I will be a joyful man
I will have a happy life
Get a job
Do my best
For the rest
Of my life

You're Beautiful Just the Way You Are
By: Keiora Sanders

If someone tells you you're ugly--
don't mind them.
You're beautiful
just the way you are.

If someone says your hair looks stupid--
ignore them.
You're beautiful
just the way you are.

If someone says your skin is too dark--
don't pay attention to them.
You're beautiful
just the way you are

Don't let anyone make you feel sad
just remember--
You're beautiful
just the way you are.

The Color of Peoples' Eyes

By: Zakiya Tucker

Don't judge people by the color of their eyes

and think they're racist or stupid

I think everyone's eyes are cute

People treat others mean because

of the color of their eyes

I think that the color

makes you unique

I wish everyone's eye color was

PINK

Black Is Beautiful
By: Tha'Resa Alexander

Why do you say
You're not beautiful?
Did someone tell you that?
Look in the mirror
You will see
A beautiful young girl.
A leader.
You should remember that your black is beautiful.
You are who you are
And no one can take that away from you.
So remember that
Your Black is Beautiful.

Summer Fun

By: Jodee M. Johnson

hot summer day

wind in my hair

jump in the pool

i don't care

NO SCHOOL

NO HOMEWORK

me and my dad

we don't have to do NO WORK

selling lemonade

gonna get paid

me and my niece play in the grass

we're wearing dresses

we got a whole lot of class

we jump in the pool

and make a BIG SPLASH

Animals

By: Kimani Nash

Animals are so cool

You might find one at the zoo

Like a tiger

That sings in a choir

That might sound funny

Just like a bunny

Jumping around with food

In his tummy

What Makes People Sad

By: Andrell Kelley

What makes people sad

Is an emotion

They have that emotion

That is what makes them sad

It makes them sad for the future

And the past

Love

By: Lashaya Tatum-Miller

Love is when

I look into your eyes

Love is when

Someone cares for another

Love is when

Someone is helping

Love is when

There is no hate

Love is you.

The Game

By: Ty'Marius Jackson

Life is a temptation of

Your will power

Your mind power

But if you don't have power

Then you won't be able to survive

In this life OR the next

You have to make the right moves

God watches over us and makes sure

We do right and not wrong

But you don't have to be perfect to play

To be honest, life is not a game

I Remember When You Said

By: Ja'Zayel Abboud

I remember when you said
I am a good person.
I remember when you said
Hi.
I remember when you said
You look good.
I remember when you said
Goodnight.
I remember when you said
Good morning.

I remember when you said
I'm leaving.

I remember when you left
Which left me in tears.

But when our mom said it's okay
I still couldn't believe that day.

I remember when you said...

A Runaway Child

By: Natalie Taylor

I sit on the curb.

Watch people walk past.

I fall asleep.

Memories flood.

Good, bad.

My mother, my dad, my siblings.

I see yelling, beating, hugging, loving.

The door.

MY LIFE.

A runaway child.

Why?

By: Nyrice Barren

Why did you leave
When I told you how I felt?

Why did you scream
When I made a mistake?

Why did you smile
When something bad happened to me?

Why, just why?
Why did you do it?

I AM A

By: Jamela Brown–Davidson

I am a book.

I am a piece of paper.

I am a pencil.

I am a teacher.

I am a kid

most of all.

Where I live

By: Landon Lazenby

I am in the 8th grade and getting F's
Because I wasn't doing my best
But I am a ball player
Shooting 3's
And
Breaking knees
I was doing the rest
But not the best
I was raised in da hood
Hearing shots
Police sirens
Looking out the window
Like
Wow. . . what happened
Police everywhere
Streets taped off. . .

It wasn't motivating,
Living in da hood.

Daylight

By: Tony Racanelli

A shiny yellow circle in the sky

Burning hot.

Why at night

Do I have to say goodbye?

When I wake

It shines in my face.

Like a crystal

From outer space.

My Destiny
By: Domonic Allen

My destiny is my future
my great life.
My destiny is my success
to have a good family.
My destiny is my education
to go to college and beyond.
My destiny is my knowledge
to go to the next level in life.
My destiny is
to be successful.

Speak To ME

By: Jaiden Beason

You see me now

You see me after

You don't say anything

I had 8 hours at school

You had 20 hours at work

But

When you come home

you still say

NOTHING TO ME

Not a, "How was your day?"

Not a, "Hello!"

Not a, "Hi!"

in the morning when you wake me up

you say, "Time to get up!"

the only time I hear you care about me

is when you say

"Bye"

I don't hear that word often

but it did feel good

I waved back and went in my school

I guess it was

just because

you were

Tired

20 hours is a long day.

Let's Unite

By: Sydney Purifoy-Mahone

Why?

Why do you have to kill?

Can't we live in happiness and not guilt?

Can we live in colors

And not black and white?

Can we unite and not fight?

Why?

Why can't we put our differences aside

And become a family tonight?

Joining together is what we need.

Can we unite and fly high in the sky?

Can we become one, you and I?

Sorrow

By: Kiyla A. Vasquez

The sorrow, yes the sorrow, I say.

Your twisted lies you tell me

Never seen you at my birthday.

Or my graduation.

As you told me you planned.

No father figure.

Only my mom and my older siblings.

The sorrow

The sorrow

You give me the sorrow.

You should be here for me.

I will not end up like you.

Not I.

The sorrow, yes, the sorrow.

Summer Fun

By: Kailyn Britton-Henning

Today the sun is shining

I ask my mom

Can we go to the water park?

She said yes!

We go in the car.

We get out of the car.

We are here!

I jump!

I splash!

In the water.

www.ingramcontent.com/pod-product-compliance
Lightning Source LLC
Chambersburg PA
CBHW051051030426
42339CB00006B/295